Guide
To
COFFEE MORNINGS
(... AFTERNOONS & EVENINGS)

JiM DAViS

RAVETTE PUBLISHING

This edition first published by Ravette Publishing Limited in 2001.

Printed and bound for Ravette Publishing Limited
Unit 3, Tristar Centre
Star Road, Partridge Green
West Sussex RH13 8RA

by Gutenberg Press Ltd, Malta.

ISBN: 1 84161 086 0

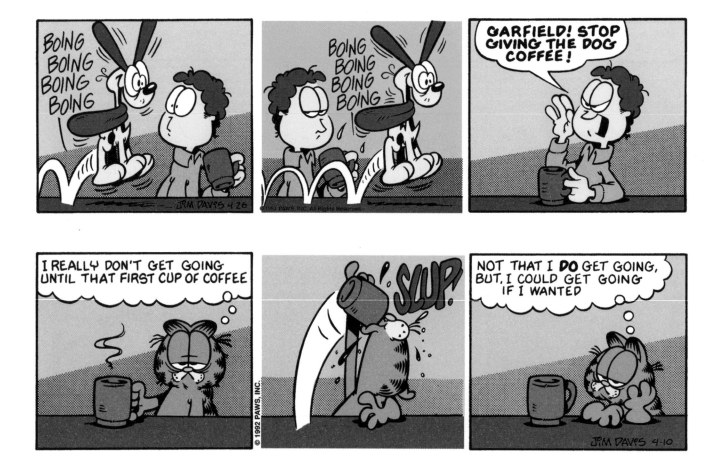